The Gnomes'
Yuletide Advent Mystery

To my children who have always given me plenty of wild story content & to children everywhere that love to work out the mysteries of the gnome world.

Melisa Nielsen has other works, including the Waldorf Essentials homeschool curriculum and the engaging stories of Super Sam the Gnome. You will also find Melisa and Erik work with parents through their program Parents Who T.H.R.I.V.E.

WaldorfEssentials.com

ParentsWhoTHRIVE.com

©Melisa Nielsen 2017   All rights reserved.

ISBN 978-1-387-39596-5

No part of this book may be reproduced in any way without the written permission from the author. She's pretty easy going, so just ask.

WaldorfEssentials.com

The Gnomes' Yuletide Advent Mystery

by Melisa Nielsen

Illustrations by Elleanor Nielsen
Edited by Erik Nielsen

Contents

Introduction	7
What is Advent?	9
Best Use of this Book	12
Part 1	18
Part 2	27
Part 3	39
Part 4	44
Part 5	51
Three Kings Day	64
References	65

Introduction

Welcome to our Advent book! This book has been many years in the making. As I have walked through my years as a parent, I am often looking for ways to streamline, yet bring more meaning to all I do. The tendency with streamlining is to make things less intimate and personal, so as I have celebrated Advent for more than 20 years as a parent and of course many more before that, I have come up with some traditions of my own. I have also walked several paths in my adult life that have served to make this time of the year richer, more engaging and have given me an ever-evolving sense of closeness to the Spirit during this time of the year.

As a young child, I was an American living in Germany. My mother was young and soaked up European culture. Advent was a cultural tradition in our home. As I got older, we converted to Catholicism and Advent was celebrated as part of our faith. As a teen I had many questions but tried to connect with Advent. As an adult, I spent some time as a Wiccan priestess and my knowledge and connections grew. In 2005, I came back to Christianity with a new outlook on the Advent season. In this book I will share my perceptions related to my journey with encouragement developing your own relationship with this very special time of the year.

Warning! The recipes I share in this book are not healthy ones! They are ones we have come to love as festival and Advent specific recipes. Several of the recipe ingredients can be substituted for healthier or allergy minded ones. Have fun and use our recipes or ones you have grown to love during this season.

What is Advent?

advent

[ad-vent] noun

1. a coming into place, view, or being; arrival: the advent of the holiday season., Dictionary.com

In the case of this book, Advent can refer to two things: 1) the arrival of Christ and 2) the coming of the sun after winter for the Northern Hemisphere or the bidding farewell to the sun for the Southern Hemisphere. Advent is traditionally observed on the four Sundays prior to Christmas or the Solstice (Winter or Summer). Often these coincide but at times they are separated by one week, because of this, planning is an important part of this festival.

What are we celebrating each week? Advent is a time of anticipation. We are anticipating the arrival that comes on that last week. In Waldorf, we focus each week on a different kingdom. Week one is the mineral kingdom. Week two, the plant. Week three, the animal, and week four, the human with the arrival of the Christ child or Child of Light for those that prefer. The focus of each week can create a paradox for some Christians, one of worshipping the creation rather than the creator, for those that struggle with this aspect, I recommend that you focus on the fruits of the Creator. Giving thanks for those fruits is not the same as worshiping them. Giving thanks shows God just how thankful we are for the beauty we have here, that has been, in Christian tradition, provided by a loving god. I personally love this time to reflect on each kingdom as it allows me to draw nearer to that which created me. It becomes a reset of sorts during a season that can be overcome with commercialism and business.

Traditions surrounding Advent are many. I have attempted to share with you some of our favorites. You might be thinking "I see these everywhere! I want to try something new!" or "Melisa has shared this with me before!" Rest assured, while I have inserted some of our favorites that we do year after year, I also have tried to include new experiences, recipes and ponderings.

Best Use of this Book

There are five parts to this story. It is a good idea to read through all the stories and the projects before you begin so that there are no surprises. There is also a handy plan sheet on the next page to help you with planning for each week.

The first part is an introduction to the mystery and the gnomes tasked to solve it. It should be given the week before Advent officially begins. You will notice that our gnomes live in the Northern Hemisphere in a land that has four seasons. I know that it is the reality of many that they do not have snow in the winter or as in the case of the Southern Hemisphere, they might be celebrating in the middle of the summer. My reality is San Diego, California. No snow. Thank goodness! For many years I lived with what many refer to as "four seasons" and I have enjoyed the challenge of connecting with the slight seasonal changes we have in our corner of the world. I encourage you to do the same. I do not change the stories to meet my surroundings, but you would be welcome to (another good reason to make a plan.) Changing the weather will not alter the story in the least, although you might prefer to change our soup suggestions to salads and our hot cocoa suggestions to a cool summer lemonade.

As I prepare our space for Advent, I like to spend the week before cleaning and arranging our nature table. I clear away the fall decorations and put them away with care. My children always help. We get out the beeswax polish and polish our candle holders. We gather any decorations we might want for our table. These decorations come out in a progression each week, allowing the anticipation to build. Part of these decorations include a beautiful wooden nativity. Each week something new appears in our nativity, with the Christ child being added on Christmas Eve.

As I prepare the space, I also begin to prepare my heart and mind. The overly commercial tendencies of the holiday season in the United States especially seem to begin spiraling out of control shortly after Halloween and it can feel like you are swimming in a sea of plastic, bad food and annoyingly loud holiday music. Preparing my mind is a process of thinking about how I want this year to feel. I consider gifts we might be giving or experiences I want to bring to our family. As I prepare my heart, I ponder the forthcoming events, the journey of Jesus' mother, the plight of all mothers caring for their unborn children. The fears and hopes we all carry, as well as the dreams we have for these children. It is during this time that I also actively state my intent for this to be a peaceful season. We review family values and begin to look at our schedule for the coming weeks. I put our sacred days on the calendar. What are your sacred days?

There is other preparation to consider. Do you have favorite menu items or treats you like to make? Will you be celebrating Saint Nicholas as well? All of these considerations are worthy of your time.

The following pages include our Advent planning sheet. Each chapter will have ideas for celebration, handwork to consider, meditations for you and a recipe to try. You might be new to Advent or just looking to include some new elements to your current traditions, either way, come along and enjoy a bit of the Advent with the Nielsen's.

Advent Plan

Dates:

Things to read & prepare:

What does this festival mean to me? What do I want to take away from celebrating it?

week 1 story:
menu items:
items to gather:
notes:

week 2 story:
menu items:
items to gather:
notes:

week 3 story:
menu items:
items to gather:
notes:

week 4 story:
menu items:
items to gather:
notes:

Part 1

Deep inside Mother Earth where the root babies sleep, the gnomes are working all year long, tending the root babies, gathering the stones, making sure all is well. All of the gnome kingdoms over the Earth work together by taking care of their own space and enjoying their own inner work of gaining wisdom. King Melchizedek, the king of the forest gnomes, was kind and wise. He led the gnomes to do their work with great care and helped them to gain all the wisdom they came to this earth to gain.

Each year the king issued a wisdom challenge to all the gnomes. The Creator picks three of the wisest gnomes to come before the king for the challenge. If they complete the challenge, they move up to help in other parts of the kingdom.

Knock, knock, knock went King Melchizedek's crystal gavel as he called the gnomes to order. "My dear brothers and sisters, please come to order. We have much business to cover on this first day of Advent."

All the gnomes filed into the great crystal meeting hall and took a seat on their amber benches. King Melchizedek gave a signal to Alpha and Omega, the wisest of the number gnomes, and all at once the space was lit to splendor, including a large beautiful pine tree adorned with beautiful lights and shapes from nature.

"Three of you have been called by our Creator to take the wisdom challenge, if you are one of these three please step forward." said the king.

Out of the corners of the hall came three gnomes, one was a boy gnome, and two young girl gnomes. The boy was William, a young gnome who was born in the forest. He was wise for his age with sandy brown hair. The girls were, Sariah and Imani, both were wise and feisty! Sariah was born in the forest, she had long golden braids. Imani was born in a land far away, she had skin dark as cocoa and wore her hair short under her gnome cap. The three approached the king, walking brave and tall. The king looked very pleased for he knew these young gnomes well, they had been wonderful at tending the root babies and had shown great potential at knowing just where to gather the prettiest of stones.

"Are you three ready for your challenge?" asked the King.

"We are," said the three as they looked at one another with excitement, remembering to also be reverent.

"Then let us begin," announced the King. "You can see our tree has many symbols from nature on it. Your first challenge is to bring me something from the mineral kingdom. It must be something that is a symbol of strength and stability."

The king excused the three from the hall to start their challenge and the remaining gnomes finished their meeting by singing winter songs.

"In the Advent garden,
Dark the night below,
Earth is waiting, waiting, waiting,
For the stars to glow."

William, Sariah and Imani walked into the forest and talked about what they were to find.

Sariah spoke first, "There are so many stones it could be! Chrysocolla is a great stone for strength but isn't known for its stability."

"Perhaps," pondered William, "we should take a walk in the night air and that will help." The girls agreed. The air was brisk and quiet. Only the owls could be heard and even they were low. It was the first night of advent, all the creatures of the Earth waited in anticipation for the Winter Solstice and the return of the sun. The days had grown so short and even though the first snow had just fallen, everyone in the forest seemed to look forward to the arrival of spring.

Imani walked meditatively and then suddenly squealed with delight. Her happy sound could be heard across the whole forest, even the trees groaned as their sleep was disturbed.

"What is it?" asked William. "Have you solved the mystery already?"

"Yes! I think I have!" she shouted. Again, the trees around her groaned as if to tell her to quiet down, but Imani was a happy gnome, she was never calm, never quiet and the trees knew they would just have to wait until she went back to her home before they would get proper rest.

"Carnelian is a perfect stone. It clears negative energy and sorrows, it protects against fear and anger and it helps to stabilize energies..." she paused and said, "My mother is always sending them to me to help me with my outbursts."

The other two gnomes giggled. They both loved Imani very much and knew that her outburst was part of who she was, she was just energetic and happy, like a butterfly jumping from task to task until she was done.

"Why don't we meet near Hematite's cave tomorrow and ask him for some guidance in mining carnelian, so we can take it to the king at our next meeting?" asked Sariah. The three gnomes agreed and parted for the evening

From our family...

A wreath is sometimes the most fun part of Advent. Since my childhood, I remember lighting the candles each week in anticipation of what was to come. Sometimes our wreaths were elaborate and sometimes simple. Recently, we have utilized a birthday ring. These are popular in Waldorf traditions and help mark seasons, holidays and birthdays. In preparation for this book, we decided to make a new wreath. Our family is changing as our older children grow up and we are looking to carry on some new things for those we are still actively walking through childhood with each day.

Wooden Advent Wreath (video available at WaldorfEssentials.com)

Materials:
1 round piece of wood, can be a fallen piece of a log, approximately 10 inches across. Ours is about 2 inches thick. We wanted to accommodate the

thickness needed to attach the screws from the candle cups.

4, 1 ¼ inch candle cups. Ours had a 5/8" hole. They also each had a hole in the bottom.

Lightly sand your surface and then cover with the watercolor design of your choice. If your piece of wood was purchased (verses fallen) as ours was, then you will want to take great care in bringing moisture back to it. We covered the surface with several coats of water before applying the paint. In hindsight, I could have soaked it in water for a few days as well.

While your wood is drying, paint your candle cups. Once everything is dry, wax with furniture wax. Use screws (or glue) and attach your candle cups.

Favorite Hot Cocoa Mix
This is a favorite here. We spent many long winters in Idaho and later Utah nursing a mug of

this cocoa. The original recipe came from Martha Stewart. I like to make this at the beginning of our Advent season and put it in a glass jar, easy for us to all get to. The kids always know that it must be winter if the cocoa is being made.

3 ½ cups sugar

2 ¼ cups cocoa

1 T salt

Mix together in a bowl and then store in an airtight container. When you are ready to make a cup, warm a cup of milk and add 2 tablespoons of the mix. Enjoy!

Part 2

The chosen gnomes were so proud of their discovery for the first part of the mystery. William, Sariah and Imani sat outside Hematite's cave waiting for an appointment with him. They wanted to ask him for help in mining some carnelian for the king. Carnelian is known for strength and stability in the mineral world and the chosen were certain Hematite would know what to do. Hematite was an odd-looking gnome, his eyes seemed to be made of crystal, he was always good at finding the best minerals and knew to lovingly take only what the gnomes needed from Mother Earth, only their portion, and leaving the rest for others to find. He was very good at his job and the gnome king had looked very favorably on him for it.

After waiting a while the three heard a familiar sound:

"With clang and clash in caverns cold
We gather glittering, gleaming gold.

With ding and dong in dark and deep
We search where silver secrets sleep.
With hey and ho in hundred homes
We mine the mountains' magic stones."

Just as he finished his little chant, Hematite turned the corner, startled by the three young gnomes, he hopped and let out a little yelp.

"What can I do for you?" he asked.

"We were wondering if you could help us with the king's challenge?" Sariah said.

"You must have figured out the king's riddle," Hematite said with a wink. "I helped him write that part!"

"We have," said Imani, "it is carnelian, but we don't know the best place to find such a wonderful stone of strength and stability. Can you help us?"

Hematite looked at the young gnomes for a while. "I'll do more than that." He said as he walked the gnomes deep into his cave. He reached above his hearth and there he had some beautiful polished pieces of carnelian. The stones were beautiful, almost red color, like the center of a ruby red grapefruit. "Take these to the gnome king," he said. "They will be a perfect addition to the great crystal hall."

Sariah kissed Hematite on the cheek and thanked him. The three gnomes took great care of the pieces until the next Advent meeting. Before long, the day arrived and they each dressed in their finest robes for the Advent meeting.

Knock, knock, knock went King Melchizedek's gavel and the excited gnomes came to order. The three chosen sat near the front and approached the king when prompted.

"Have you solved the first mystery my young gnomes?" he asked.

"We have," remarked William "a stone that is both strong and stable is carnelian." William said as Imani and Sariah curtsied and passed the stones to the king. The king examined them and then walked over to a nearby table that was covered in a beautiful white silk to mark the falling snow and placed the stones in the center of the table.

"Well done!" exclaimed the gnome king. "You are ready for your second challenge. For this second part, you must bring me something from the plant world that is a symbol of great growth, strength and is changeable."

The chosen three were excited with their new task. They were excused from the gathering to begin their work. As they departed, the rest of the gnomes chanted a winter verse together in preparation for a visit from the great Saint Nicholas.

"Upon his snow white steed
With wind and lightening speed
St. Nicholas leaves the sky
And comes a riding by."

The gnomes found themselves walking through the forest again so the night air could help them with the challenge.

"There are so many plants that could fit this riddle" said William as the three strolled in the moonlight.

"Sunflower... mandrake...carrot...oh fiddle dee dee," said Sariah, "there are so many possibilities. We all tended root babies, what do you think it could be Imani?"

Imani was pacing the forest floor mumbling… "growth, strength, changeability…"

This time it was William to burst forth… "I know what it is! It can't be just a flower or vegetable, it has to be a tree!" Just as he shouted, the trees groaned for him too. Would there be no peace until this challenge is over the Mighty Oak thought to himself?

"All plants grow," William continued, "they all have a cycle, some flower in spring and die off in the autumn, some flower in early winter, few flowers stay alive all year long, some die completely and give themselves to the earth to be born again as something else, others come back in the new year, some are even strong, but trees… trees are strong, so many gnomes and humans build with them, they also show a great deal of growth, even when entire forests are burned, trees find a way to adapt and grow, and they are changeable, they stay alive all year, only their leaves and flowers fall off, the tree continues to be alive, even now, I hear them groan as they sleep."

Sariah and Imani congratulated William and started thinking about what they could take to the king for the nature table in the crystal hall. Of course a full grown tree would be too big for them. They decided that a trip to visit the queen was in order, for she is none other than Mother Nature. She is so sacred that she is rarely spoken to, but the three wise gnomes knew she would know just what to bring her husband, King Melchizedek. The gnomes went deep into the gnome caverns where they knew the great Mother would be resting and quietly knocked at her door.

"Come in my children," called the queen. "What brings you so deep within the Earth?"

"Well," began Imani "we are the chosen gnomes and we are working on the second part of the mystery.

We decided that the answer was a tree, but we wondered just how we could bring something so large to the king."

"Oh my dears, I know just who you are, for I have been watching, silently watching..." began the queen, "take this token to my husband, he will be pleased." And with that the Mother handed the gnomes a tiny sapling, it was just out of infancy and ready to take shape with the coming spring. "I appoint you three to watch over this sapling and to make sure it gains a proper place in the forest in the coming months."

"Oh thank you great mother!" they chanted together as they each gave her a hug and quietly left the cavern to let the great mother continue to rest.

They all knew the gnome king would be impressed with their finding. Sariah agreed to take the sapling home and look after it until the next Advent meeting.

From our family...

Stones have always meant something to me. I remember purchasing my first "worry rock" as a teen and after that, I always kept some sort of stone or shell near me. As an adult, I grew fond of different stones. I was always drawn to the amethyst, my birth stone, and was fascinated by the peace they seemed to bring me. In my Pagan years, I collected many stones and when I came back to Christianity, I feared I would have to hide that part of me – the part of me that knew stones carried healing powers. As I asked in prayer what was the best thing to do, I was reminded that all good things come from the same place. Stones are very much a part of my life today. We use them on our home nature table, carry them in pockets to soothe our worries or even simply to be used as a key – a reminder that things are going to be okay.

Carnelian Grid

Materials:

6" circular wooden plate

1 carnelian stone

5 quartz points

Compass

Pencils

Glue

This is a fun and easy project. The hardest part is drawing the star! We have included a geometry video to help with the process. Once you have drawn your star and painted your wooden plate, arrange your stones with the carnelian in the center and the quartz points, pointing out. Glue the stones in place using the smallest amount of glue possible. Let dry overnight.

If the grid doesn't interest you, perhaps take some time to just focus on the Christmas star. This is the star that would lead the magi to the newborn king, the child of Light, the chosen one. Emmanuel. As we begin our Advent, we always take some time to talk about the preparations the Wise Men must have been making for their journey to see Jesus.

My Great Grandma's Sugar Cookies

I have given this recipe out before. It is a family favorite. I often imagine what my great-grandmother will say when I see her on the other side. It will either be "Melisa Dawn, I am so glad you shared that with everyone!" or "Melisa Dawn! What were you thinking?!"

1 cup shortening (Grandma used lard)
2 cups sugar
2 eggs
1 cup buttermilk
4-5 cups + flour
½ t. salt
1 t. baking soda
2 t. baking powder

Cream shortening, sugar and eggs. Add buttermilk. Sift salt, baking soda and baking powder with 1 cup of the flour. Add to mixture. Add remaining flour.

Mix until it can be worked by hand then roll out and cut or drop by spoonful on a cookie sheet. Bake at 375° for 10 minutes. Suitable for royal icing.

Part 3

Knock, knock, knock went the gavel of King Melchizedek and all the gnomes came to order. They all noticed a familiar visitor in the great cavern – St. Nicholas! He often came to rest with the gnomes after his journey around the world. The three chosen sat near the front and when prompted, came to stand before the king.

"Your highness," began William, "we have brought you the symbol from the plant world that is strong, changeable and full of growth." He handed the king the small pot containing the sapling they had all cared for over the last week.

King Melchizedek was so pleased with the young gnomes. He turned to St. Nicholas and saw the smile on his face as well

"I see you have been to see our Mother," said the king. "I trust she is resting comfortably."

"She is," said Sariah "she was kind enough to give us this sapling to care for until the spring comes and it is ready to be planted in the ground."

The king took the beautiful sapling and placed it on the table near the stones and then turned back to the gnomes.

"Your next task is a bit harder. This time you must find something from the animal world. This again must be strong but also have the ability to give life and food from the same source. Good luck my young gnomes. You have nearly completed all your tasks." With that the King turned to the rest of the gnomes and broke out in song.

"In the Christmas garden,
Where we singing go,
Life is glowing, flowing, glowing,
Red the roses grow."

The three wise gnomes were tired and decided they would meet in the forest to start the new riddle the next day.

From our family...

I love plants, but I am the first one to say that I am a bad plant mommy! In fact, when I get all excited about planting a garden, my family generally says "Mom, why are you doing that? Homicide is a crime!" I am really good at raising children, plants, not so much. Living in San Diego though has brought to me a love of plants that are hard to kill! Succulents to my rescue!

Glass Terrarium

Materials:

Small glass bowl or jar
Sand
Sea shells or rocks
Small succulent cutting

Succulents need a sandy soil and do well in many small environments as long as you don't make the jar or bowl too moist. Layer your sand in and then your rocks or sea shells around your cutting. Lightly water. Place in a well-lit place in your home and enjoy.

Apple Pudding

This recipe was lovingly given by my ex-husband's grandmother. She was an amazing woman who drank a Dr. Pepper daily, ate bacon fat and loved to cook for those around her. May God rest her soul.

In a bowl combine:
1 cup flour (can use gluten free flour)
1 t. baking soda
1 t. cinnamon
¾ t. nutmeg
½ t. salt

In another bowl combine:
½ cup butter

½ white sugar

½ brown sugar

1 egg

Add 4 cups diced apples and nuts (optional)

Bake in a pan at 350° for 45 minutes.

Part 4

Imani was the first to get to the forest clearing on that bright winter morning. She saw the hens roaming free in the forest and got some corn from her pocket (that she kept there just for these lovely hens) and started to throw it out for them. Soon after, the other two gnomes came and pulled corn from their pockets doing the same. They silently fed the hens for a while and then Sariah started talking.

"I have been thinking about this challenge the whole night and I am stuck."

The other two gnomes nodded in deep thought. They continued to feed the hens when Daisy, a friendly fat, orange Brakel hen, came by to get some corn.

"Cluck, what's wrong, cluck, cluck?" asked Daisy.

"We are the chosen gnomes this year, and we are stuck on one of the king's riddles," said William.

"Cluck, what's the riddle?"

William almost didn't tell her, for he knew hens could be clever but he wasn't sure she could help.

"The king asked us to look for something in the animal kingdom that is strong and can give life and food, there is nothing like that – I thought of a cow but I don't think that is it," William explained.

Daisy chuckled and clucked. "Follow me," she said to the gnomes.

The three gnomes were curious now and all began to follow her. She led them back to her nest that was in the branches of a mighty fir tree. "Here," she said as she gestured to Sariah to take an egg.

"But this is an egg, your egg, don't you need it?" questioned Imani.

"Oh dear me, I lay so many eggs each year, if they all hatched I would not know what to do with myself! I have always freely given my eggs to the gnome kingdom as you have all been so good to take care of us and let us roam free in the forest. Red, my rooster, helps me with the ones we plan to hatch, the others would simply go to waste," said Daisy.

The three gnomes realized Daisy was more clever than they had thought, she gave them something with a strong outer shell and inside was the potential for life or for food. She also gave them one of her feathers to put on the nature table.

"From this," Daisy pointed at the egg "comes this." Daisy points to the feather. "Cluck, hens lay a strong shell that gives both life and food. Give my best to the king." Daisy said.

William agreed to keep the egg in a cold place until the next meeting, Imani took the feather and agreed to care for it.

Knock, knock, knock went the king's gavel. The king was calling the next meeting to order and the gnomes all took their places. When it was time, the chosen three came forward.

"What have you brought us of the animal world?" asked King Melchizedek.

"Oh kind and dear king, we have brought you a treasure from the animal world," said Imani as she placed the egg in the hands of the king. "It is strong and was given freely by the hen, Daisy, as a symbol of both life and food. She also was kind enough to give us one of her feathers for our nature table."

King Melchizedek was so pleased — he knew they were near the end of their tasks. "Well done!" he said beaming from ear to ear (under his beard of course!)

"Young gnomes, your final mystery to solve is one that will test your wit and wisdom and is the key to peace in all the earth, both below in our kingdom and above where the humans live. We will meet again under the sky for the solstice celebration. Have the mystery solved by then. For now, dance and enjoy yourselves! It is the last week of Advent!"

With that all the gnomes cheered and began their party.

From our family...

For many years we lived in a cold weather environment and I always worried about the birds. Between our cat hunting them and the freakishly cold winters, I was continually looked for something to keep the birds happy. From peanut butter pine cones rolled in bird seed, to homemade suet in thrift store mugs, our birds were happy!

Recycled Mug Birdfeeders

Materials:

Old coffee mugs
½ pounds of lard
1 cup crunchy peanut butter
1 cup dried fruit
3-4 cups bird seed

Melt the lard and the peanut butter together. Add the dried fruit and seeds. Pour into mugs and cool in the refrigerator. Hang from trees in your yard.

Millet Cake

This recipe can easily be made with gluten free flour. You can substitute the orange juice for another juice or even water.

2 cups flour
1 t. baking soda
1 t. baking powder
½ t. salt
1 ½ cups cooked millet
1 cup orange juice
½ cup water
1/3 cup coconut oil
½ cup maple syrup
2 t. vanilla
2 eggs

Preheat oven at 350°. Oil and flour two 8" pans or a 9x13" pan. Sift the dry ingredients and set aside. In a blender place millet and orange juice, blend. At water, oil and syrup. Blend. Add the rest of the wet ingredients. Combine with the dry. Pour into pans and bake for 30-40 minutes.

Part 5

It was the day before Yule and the chosen three were struggling to know the answer to the final riddle given to them by the king. Knowing the wisdom of the great Mother, the three went to visit her again. She would be awake today, getting ready for the solstice celebration — the three gnomes were sure that she could assist them. They all entered the Queen's cave in a reverent manner.

"Good morning my children," the Queen greeted them. "What can I help you with?"

"Oh great Mother" began Imani "we have been trying to solve the last riddle and we have had no luck, tomorrow is the solstice and we have nothing to bring to the king."

"Young and wise gnomes," began the Queen "did you think to pray?"

The three gnomes shook their heads in shame. "Well then," said the Queen "I think you have your answer."

The gnomes left the Queen's cave and headed to the mushroom doorway. They knew there was a special grove in the trees where they should go to offer up a prayer to the Creator. Once there, William offered up the prayer, asking the Creator to help them to answer the last riddle. Suddenly there was a bright light and a song from the heavens.

Angels sang:

"Seven angels at the door of heaven,
Light and bright.
Seven angels at the door of heaven,
Holding a light.
Open your heart to the light so bright,
Open your heart to the angels in white."

The gnomes looked toward the heavens and one of the angels spoke:

"You have done a wonderful thing coming to the Creator for help. The answer you seek is near. Come with us and we will show you a great vision."

Silently the three gnomes followed the angels. They beheld a beautiful young woman and cradled in her arms a baby. An angel said:

"Behold, this child is capable of great things, he is known as the Prince of Peace, the Messiah, the Son, the Sun, he is born in the dark of the shortest night, he is love, some call him Horus, some Jesus, he has many names. Your king Melchizedek will know him as the Anointed One."

Suddenly the gnomes were back in the grove of trees and the angels were gone. Sariah searched her bag for a drawing pad and pencils, she quickly sketched what they had seen. She made a beautiful picture of the mother and child for the king and wrote on it "The Anointed One."

The gnomes were silent for the remainder of the day, meditating on what they had seen. They agreed to meet by the mushroom doorway before the solstice celebration.

The air was cold as the gnomes from the entire gnome kingdom filed into the forest, hundreds of gnomes — number gnomes, root gnomes, mining gnomes, carpentry gnomes, animal gnomes and many more. King Melchizedek stood on the high rock and knocked the ground three times with his cane for them to all come to order. Next to him stood the queen, the great Mother Earth herself, dressed white as the driven snow with long hair, black as the night. The gnomes all came to order.

"Where are the chosen ones?" asked the king

"We are here your Highness," answered William, Sariah, and Imani from the back of the crowd.

All at once the sea of gnomes parted and the three stepped forward. There was confusion among the gnomes as all the three carried with them was a piece of paper that appeared to be in a beautifully crafted wooden frame.

The king addressed the young gnomes "Have you found for me a symbol from the human world that can bring peace to all?"

"We have," said Sariah as she presented the king with the frame. "Your Highness, we were very troubled by this challenge and it took much pondering and eventual prayer for us to find the answer. We were certain we could do this challenge on our own but we found that once we allowed the

Creator to help us then we were given a great gift. The gift of a vision from angels." She turned to Imani.

"In the vision we saw something wonderful. We beheld a woman fair holding a child. The angel told us that the child was known by many names but that you would know him as The Anointed One. We were told that the child had the ability to bring peace to all if only they would allow it." Hannah said.

"Well done, well done!" boasted the king, he was so proud of his gnomes. "You have completed the challenge."

The crowd parted again as another king stepped into the moonlight. It was King Equals, ruler over the number gnomes. He was dressed in white with a golden crown and a gold equals sign on his cape.

"You gnomes have been chosen by the Creator to move forward into the sacred world of numbers," started Equals. "I would be honored if you would come to my kingdom and train with my gnomes."

The three gnomes danced with glee and accepted the invitation. All at once the solstice party began and the forest floor was alive with merriment. Just before sunrise the gnomes gathered together once more to watch together the dawn of the new season, the birth of the Sun.

The End.

From our family....

This last week of Advent is so precious to us. We love to celebrate the Light! We bring out all our lanterns, often make new ones, have fun making window stars and bake a birthday cake for Jesus. It is a fun time in our home. While it is the focal point of the season for many families, as parents we often discuss it as part of the greater whole. The birth of Jesus or the Child of Light is our reminder to bring our own light to the world. We also reflect on our family during this time. It can be fun to draw a family tree together as a visual, especially for young children. They really do not understand the passage of generations or the concept of ancestors in an abstract spoken way until they are older than seven. The passage of time concepts really begin to stir around age nine. For young children, they need to see pictures. Pull out pictures of your childhood and talk about traditions you had as a family. Talk about how your family came to live where they do. Have fun with this time of the year. Slow down and vow to be meaningful in all you do.

Small Jar Lanterns

Materials:

Small glass jars, we really like the small ones that you can get yogurt in, the size is perfect.

Kite paper or tissue paper

White glue

Sponge brush or some sort of means to spread the glue

Water down your glue a bit so that it is easy to spread with a brush. Make small designs with your kite paper or just tear pieces at random. Brush a foundation layer of glue on your glass jar and then place your shapes on top. Cover your jar with your design and then place a thin layer of your glue mixture on top. Allow 12 hours to dry. Once dry, place a tea light inside and enjoy the light!

Happy Birthday Jesus Cake

We make this cake as a treat for Christmas Eve. My mother made it when I was a child in Germany and it is a celebration favorite at all birthdays.

You can use any sponge cake or angel food cake recipe for this. Bake it in a jelly roll pan or cookie sheet. Make real, fresh whipped cream for the filling, spread mandarin oranges on the cream. Next, roll up your cake like a log. Top with whipped cream and more oranges.

A variation might be to make a Yule log cake instead. For this we infuse hazelnut spread into the whipped cream for the color and omit the oranges. We might decorate it with mushrooms from marzipan or meringue.

Bread Pudding with Carmel Sauce

This is a special breakfast favorite of ours. I love to make it in the crock pot so it is ready when we get up on Christmas morning. I don't have to step away from having fun to cook. Alternatively, growing up my mother always made (and still makes) a soufflé for Christmas morning. I am including both recipes.

8 cups of cubed bread – I keep a container in my freezer for bread ends just for this!
2 cups of milk
4 eggs
¼ cup of sugar
¼ cup of butter
½ t. vanilla
¼ t. nutmeg
¼ t. cinnamon
You can also add raisins.

Put bread in the crock pot (you can also use an Instant Pot on the slow cooker setting.) Mix together all other ingredients and pour over the bread. Toss and let sit for 15 minutes. Then cook, overnight on low or start it first thing in the morning on a higher setting and it will be ready in a few hours.

For the sauce:

½ cup butter
½ cup white sugar
½ cup brown sugar

½ cup whipping cream
1 t. vanilla

Put all ingredients EXCEPT vanilla in a pot and bring to a boil, melting everything together. Once it is a rolling boil, remove from heat and add the vanilla. Cool and serve with your bread pudding. Save some for ice cream and other treats.

Grandma Pam's Breakfast Soufflé

8 slices of bread, cubed
1 ½ pound of browned sausage
2 cups of shredded cheddar cheese
Butter 9x13 inch pan. Line with bread, then cheese, then sausage.

Mix together and set aside:
2 ½ cups milk
¾ t dry mustard
4 beaten eggs

Mix and add to liquid mixture:

1 can cream of mushroom soup

½ cup milk

Pour over layers and let stand overnight in refrigerator. Bake uncovered at 300° for 90 minutes.

Three Kings Day

I can't write a book about Advent without talking about Three Kings Day or 12th Night. This is a very important part of the Christian celebration of Advent. It is a celebration of the day the Wise Men or Magi came to visit Christ. As a festival, we play king for a day, tell the story of the Magi and bake! Of course, baking! As you look toward this important part of the Christmas season, take the time to look within. Are you a Magi or a Wise Man or Woman? What gifts do you bring? Share together what your hopes and dreams are for the coming years. What strengths do you have that you would like to add to? What goals do you have that you would like to see this coming year? This festival is for the Nielsen's an official start to our new year.

References

The Wynstones Press books have long been a favorite of mine and have shaped the way I bring festivals to my children. They are filled with stories, songs and poems that are appropriate for the seasons. These books are titled for the seasons.

Wynstones Press, Winter

Support for this book along with videos and cards for your nature table can be found here:

https://www.waldorfessentials.com/support-gnomes-yuletide-advent-mystery/

Made in the USA
Las Vegas, NV
01 December 2023